BANKRUPTCY
THE LAW OF HOPE

How to Use Bankruptcy
as a Springboard to a
Brighter Financial Future

MARSHALL M. SLAYTON, ESQ.

questions@marshallslayton.com
434-205-9035

PZNAPOD PRESS
Charlottesville, Virginia

Bankruptcy – The Law of Hope
Marshall M. Slayton, Esq
PZNAPOD Press
Copyright © 2018 by Marshall M. Slayton
Cover Design: Fran Cannon Slayton
Fran Cannon Slayton, Editor

While the author of this book is a lawyer authorized to practice in
the state of Virginia, he is not your lawyer and no attorney-client
privilege has been created by virtue of you reading or using this
book. While care was taken to ensure accuracy, the information in
this book does not, and is not intended to, constitute legal advice;
instead, all information in this book is for general informational,
educational, and promotional purposes only. No warranty may be
created or extended by sales or promotional materials.
Information in this book may not constitute the most up-to-date
legal or other information. Readers of this book should hire their
own experienced attorney to obtain advice with respect to any
particular legal matter. No reader should act or refrain from acting
on the basis of information in this book without first seeking legal
advice from counsel in the relevant jurisdiction. Only your
individual attorney can provide assurances that the information
contained herein – or your interpretation of it – is applicable or
appropriate to your particular situation. The views expressed
herein are those of the author writing in his individual capacity
only. All liability with respect to actions taken or not taken based
on the contents of this book are hereby expressly disclaimed. The
content in this book is provided "as is;" no representations are
made that the content is error-free.

ISBN: 978-1-7329554-0-0

Printed in the United States of America by Author2Market

INTRODUCTION

WHY BANKRUPTCY IS THE LAW OF HOPE

If you are reading this book, the crushing burden of debt may be something that's in the forefront of your mind right now. Perhaps you are behind on your mortgage payments. Maybe your wages are being garnished. Or you may be one of the many people in the United States today who are recently divorced, have incurred unexpected medical bills, or have suffered a recent layoff at your job. Perhaps you've been "getting by" using credit cards to pay your regular monthly expenses, just to make ends meet. There are many, many reasons that regular people find themselves struggling with their finances in today's world.

I'm here to tell you: you're not alone. According to Northwest Mutual's *2018 Planning and Progress Study*, average personal debt in America exceeded $38,000 in 2018 (and that's *excluding* mortgage debt). Fifty-three percent of Americans cited reducing debt as their number one financial priority. And two out of every ten people spend a staggering 50-100% of their income each month just trying to pay off what they owe. No wonder so many people feel like they can't get ahead – it's because they are falling further and further behind.

My name is Marshall M. Slayton, and I am the owner of Slayton Law, PLC, a law firm in Charlottesville, Virginia specializing exclusively in debt relief and bankruptcy law. During my quarter century career as a lawyer, I've helped literally thousands of people move beyond their burdensome financial situations using what I have come to call "The Law of Hope" - the Federal Bankruptcy Code of the United States.

When I was a child, my own family experienced the emotional ups and downs caused by financial instability, so I understand on a very personal level the anxiety and stress it causes. As a result, I have great respect and great empathy for each person who walks into my law firm looking for a way to solve their own financial problems.

For these people I have a clear message: you have great reasons to be hopeful! It is possible to move through and beyond your current financial problems – I have seen it happen with my own clients time and time again. To achieve this, you must begin by educating yourself about ALL your financial options – including how you can use Federal bankruptcy law to your own advantage. And once you have educated yourself, you must commit to taking proactive steps so you can protect your – and your family's – future.

In this book, I lay out options for people who are struggling with debt. I talk about the pros and cons of debt negotiation and credit counseling, but most of all I describe how regular people can use the United States Bankruptcy laws to protect their assets, stamp out their debt, and start down the road to a brighter financial future.

Sadly, bankruptcy has been stigmatized in our society to the point where the very people it could most benefit are hesitant to find out how it could help them. This is unfortunate and unnecessary, because the Constitution itself provides for bankruptcy laws in our country to help people to keep their homes, their vehicles, and their retirement savings when hard economic times hit. The purpose of these laws is to help people not only weather the storm, but also to come out on the other side ready and able to create a new future and a new success story for themselves and their families.

Many very famous – and very rich – people have used our country's bankruptcy laws to overcome hard times and to protect and increase their wealth. There is no reason that regular people should not take advantage of this same protection as well.

The United States bankruptcy laws are not laws of failure and misery – they are laws of hope that you can use to arrive at a brighter tomorrow. May this book give you hope in the midst of your own financial struggles.

Sincerely,
Marshall M. Slayton
Slayton Law, PLC
Charlottesville, Virginia
Phone: 434-205-9035
November 29, 2018

TABLE OF CONTENTS

Introduction: Why Bankruptcy is The Law of Hope   i

Chapter 1: Reasons to Hope   1

Chapter 2: Will I Lose My House?   15

Chapter 3: Help - I'm Being Foreclosed!   22

Chapter 4: Will I Lose My Car?   29

Chapter 5: What About My Credit Score?   33

Chapter 6: Debt Negotiation Agencies   36

Chapter 7: Credit Counseling   47

Chapter 8: Is Bankruptcy Right for Me?   50

Chapter 9: Should I File Myself?   52

Chapter 10: Philosophical Objections   59

Chapter 11: Chapter 7 or Chapter 13?   64

Chapter 12: Protecting Your Retirement   71

Chapter 13: Protecting Your Privacy   73

Chapter 14: Bye-Bye Harassing Calls!   76

Chapter 15: Help - I've Been Garnished!   78

Chapter 16: What About My IRS Debt?   81

Chapter 17: The Slayton Law Advantage   83

Chapter 18: Your Next Steps   99

Index: 100

CHAPTER 1

REASONS TO HOPE

When I was young, before I went to law school, I knew a number of people – some in my own family – who were touched by huge financial challenges. These were good, hardworking people who, through bad luck or careless error, found themselves struggling to make ends meet.

Their financial problems affected other areas of their lives as well, causing stress, tears, embarrassment, the breakdown of relationships, and even depression.

When I was a child, my own family lived the roller coaster of emotion caused by financial stress. My father was a smart man, but he had a hard time keeping a job. Sometimes he made very good money. But just as often we were drinking powdered milk at home or were putting back groceries in the checkout line of the supermarket because my mother did not have enough money to pay for them at the end of the month.

My grandparents, too, lived on this same financial roller coaster. My grandfather "made deals" and the money was good when he was a young man. But as he got older, the deals didn't happen as often, and they eventually stopped all together. When his last deal went south he fell deeply into debt. He wasn't sure what to do about it, so he ignored the problem. Eventually, my grandparents' home fell into total disrepair. I'll never forget visiting them one snowy winter night when I discovered they were keeping their spare bedroom at a temperature of about 40 degrees. It was so cold I couldn't stay warm under the covers. They were trying to save money.

Seeing people I loved in such a state left an indelible impression on me and, in retrospect, greatly influenced my decision to become a bankruptcy attorney.

If you've been touched by a financial crisis or you've seen a loved one dragged through the financial ringer as I have, chances are you will recognize some of the situations I will be describing in this book. To protect privacy, these are not particular stories of actual clients, but are representative composites of many types of difficult financial situations I've experienced with many of my bankruptcy clients and others who chose not to file bankruptcy throughout the years.

Take John and Bernice, for example. They had just closed on their dream house and moved in with their twin five-year-olds and pet Golden Retriever, Annie, when two devastating setbacks hit them within just eight days. First, Bernice, the primary breadwinner, wrenched her back while unpacking a heavy box from the move and found herself out of work for six months. Then, John discovered that his business partner had cheated a vendor, who decided to sue for six figures. John hadn't yet set up a corporate entity for his partnership, so suddenly all his personal assets were at stake.

John and Bernice had to confront the very real possibility that they'd lose their house and have to move back in with Bernice's mother.

Or what about Alice, a 72-year-old retired worker who, after tragically losing her partner of 40 years to cancer, was victimized by insurance fraud, which depleted her savings and effectively wiped out her safety net?

Or consider Brianna, a 26-year-old entrepreneur, who racked up $50,000 in credit card debt trying to get her online business off the ground. Barely able to keep up with the monthly payments, she developed crippling anxiety from the constant harassing calls from debt collectors.

I became a bankruptcy attorney to serve people like these – good, hard-working people who've found themselves in painful circumstances that they never dreamed they'd face, unsure how to get free, and frightened at the prospect of a future filled with stress, embarrassment, and no way to get ahead.

My 25 years of experience as a bankruptcy attorney allows me to guide my clients on a journey from paralyzing financial pain and fear to having real hope and a fresh start in life. Time and time again, I see the relief on their faces as they come to my office and take their first step to begin this journey – because from that moment on, they know they will no longer be facing their financial troubles alone. Could there possibly be a more fulfilling job?

During my career, I've:

- Represented literally thousands of clients and helped them get rid of millions upon millions of dollars' worth of debt.
- Been rated a "Preeminent" attorney – the highest award possible – by my legal peers.

- Been rated a "Superb" and "Client's Choice" attorney on Avvo.

- Taught continuing legal education courses on bankruptcy to other lawyers for the Virginia State Bar.
- Published a number of articles for lawyers on various aspects of bankruptcy.

I know and understand bankruptcy law. But I've also learned that being a successful and effective bankruptcy attorney requires more than knowledge – it's also an art. It requires having the skills and temperament to identify and deploy the right strategies at the right time to fight off creditors and protect essential assets.

Additionally, I understand that the very best bankruptcy attorneys – the ones who are able to give real hope to their clients – have one more essential ingredient: the ability to empathize and connect with their clients on a human level – the ability to simply listen.

When was the last time you were just listened to?

My clients have been through truly heartrending situations. I am proud that my own life experiences with difficult situations now help me to provide them with the advice, connection, and reassurance they need. I truly care about my clients. I want to give them hope. I want to help them get the fresh start they need.

Why do I have a passion for helping people with their financial problems?

Every day I come to work is a blessing. I get to meet hardworking, genuine, and dedicated people who are stuck in debt, but who I know also have great cause to be hopeful. When my clients come to me they are in pain. They are ashamed that they can't pay their bills. They are frustrated that they can't support their families and give their children the lives they deserve. They have social anxiety, dreading upcoming high school reunions or chance encounters with their exes at the supermarket. And they are exhausted from the harassing calls and frightening letters from creditors.

Like my own family did at times, many of my clients live in a perpetual touch-and-go state. Financially, it's month-to-month or sometimes even day-to-day.

That I know ways to relieve their financial pain, stop the harassing phone calls, and reclaim their natural dignity makes what I do both an honor and a privilege. It's why I get up the morning. And it's why everyone in my office works hard at what they do.

What I do in a nutshell: Offer good people a release from the stress, shame, fear and uncertainty caused by their financial problems.

When my clients first come into my office to see me, they often experience instant relief at that very first meeting. Why? It's not necessarily because of anything I say or do – the strategies I lay out for them, or the action plan we develop together. Rather, the relief comes because I sit there and listen attentively.

In my opinion, people these days are starved for empathy – for the need to "feel heard." This is especially true for folks who've been through the wringer, who've confronted

demons in multiple areas of their lives –
financial, medical, relational, psychological,
and spiritual.

I listen to them and just let them share their
stories. I always keep a box of tissues handy,
because this cathartic retelling often leads
spontaneously to tears. These are the tears of
finally being able to express oneself fully
after months or years of holding back and
"sucking it up" to put on a brave face to the
world.

All too often, when people come to others for
help with problems, the response tends to be
intellectual and distant. And yes, at some
point, we will need to get to the nuts and
bolts of solving the problem. But first, the
person in pain needs to feel understood.

If you're raising two kids at home with
another on the way, and you're knee-deep in
credit card debt, and then you get into a car
accident… sure, you want practical insight
about what to do. But you also need someone

just to acknowledge the scope of your challenge. And when I do that, I immediately notice a shift and a sense of release, because my clients know they're no longer dealing with their problems alone.

Slayton Law: A Hopeful Approach

I've practiced bankruptcy law for a quarter of a century and have served literally thousands of clients in that time. My clients have dealt with almost every conceivable financial problem – which means that I have dealt with almost every conceivable financial problem, too.

Whenever I meet with a new client, I see a unique human being who happens to be going through a tough time right now – and I am grateful that I have the expertise and ability to guide them through that tough time. I know I can give them hope by showing them their options, helping them build a pathway out of their maze, and being by their side as they get to a better place.

When I meet with a new client, I don't just see a person in pain – I see a person who is taking the first step toward moving beyond that pain.

Bankruptcy law is complicated – that's why so few lawyers practice it, and why even fewer lawyers choose it as their exclusive area of practice, as I do. Bankruptcy is not a type of law that is easy to just "dabble" in.

Bankruptcy law is all I do – and this is one reason my clients feel hopeful when they meet with me. They realize that I know the bankruptcy laws inside and out, backwards and forwards, with my eyes open and with my eyes closed. They understand that I am one of the very few bankruptcy attorneys in Central Virginia who has been awarded the highest "Preeminent" Martindale-Hubbell rating by my legal peers. And I believe they are proud that their lawyer has the highest rating possible by clients on Avvo – a 10.

When people come into my office, my experience, awards, and ratings are part of what gives them hope that their own situation is going to get better. They know they've made a good choice to find out more about their options by scheduling a free consultation with me.

Let me put it to you this way: if you had to have a complicated surgery, would you choose a surgeon who only did that kind of surgery once every few months, or one who performed it multiple times a day, every single day of his life? You'd choose the surgeon who does it every day. Why? Because experience matters.

Similarly, as you choose an attorney to help you navigate your financial challenges, it's important to pick one who has the knowledge, experience, and compassion to see you through.

At Slayton Law, it is our calling and privilege to end creditor harassment, get rid of debt, and rekindle hope in our clients. Anyone can find themselves in a difficult financial situation at any time in life. In our office, we strive to understand – to listen – with compassion, empathy, and most of all, with respect. Most of all, we do what we do because we firmly believe that everyone deserves to be hopeful; everyone deserves to know their options; everyone deserves a fresh start.

CHAPTER 2

WILL I LOSE MY HOUSE?

Happily, the answer I most often give my bankruptcy clients is most often a resounding:

No, you don't have to lose your house!

Take Barbara, for example. Barbara is a widow who owns her own home and pays her mortgage faithfully every month. She doesn't have any equity in her home – meaning that if she sold it she would be able to pay off her mortgage but would make no additional profits from the sale.

When Barbara's son, Larry, lost his job two years ago, Barbara agreed to co-sign a loan so he could buy a car to drive to and from his new job. When Larry lost that job, too, and stopped being able to make payments on the car, it was repossessed and sold for far less than what Larry owed on it. Because Barbara had co-signed the note, the creditor came after her for the $20,000 balance – a large amount of money that she can't afford to pay if she's to keep current on her mortgage payments.

She comes to me to find out all her options.

When I first meet with Barbara in my office, she's not very hopeful. The first question she has for me is this: can I keep my house?

I am happy to be able to tell her the answer is YES, Barbara, there's a way you can keep your house!

When a person owns her own home but does not have much equity in it (that is, would not make a profit from the sale of the house after paying off the mortgage), she can usually file a Chapter 7 Bankruptcy to get rid of her debt, while still keeping her house.

How is this possible? When there is no equity in a house, the Chapter 7 Trustee can't sell it and make any additional profit to help pay off the owner's other debts. Selling the house wouldn't help creditors get any of their money back and would just put the debtor in the position of having to find another place to live. For this reason, selling the house does not make any financial sense.

So, as long as Barbara keeps current on her mortgage while she's in bankruptcy, she can keep her house.

This is why filing bankruptcy works for people like Barbara.

But What if I Have Equity in My House? Can I Keep It Then?

Happily (again), the answer to this question is often a resounding:

Yes!

In situations where a person has equity in her home – that is, would make a profit from the

17

sale of the house after the mortgage is paid off – I often suggest that she file a Chapter 13 Bankruptcy rather than a Chapter 7 Bankruptcy. Why? Let me explain using the following scenario.

Meet Jane. Jane's situation is the same as Barbara's – she is a widow who co-signed on a loan for a relative and wound up owing a $20,000 debt she could not afford to pay, in addition to her own mortgage payment.

But, unlike Barbara, Jane has $20,000 of equity in her home – that is, if Jane sold her house and then paid off the mortgage, she would make an additional $20,000 from the sale.

Jane could sell her house, move all her belongings out, and use the $20,000 in profit to pay off the debt. But then she would have to find another place to live, lose her home and all the memories it holds of her deceased spouse, and also lose her largest asset – one she could otherwise have passed on to her children upon her death.

A friend of Jane's who has a son who is a first-year law school student, told Jane that if she files bankruptcy when she has $20,000 of equity in her home the Trustee will just sell Jane's house and use the $20,000 of equity to pay off Jane's debt – so she'll lose her home. And it's true, if Jane filed a Chapter 7 bankruptcy, this is exactly what would happen. Jane would lose her home.

Fortunately, that's not what happens because Jane decides to come into my office to make sure she understands ALL her options. When she comes in to meet me, I advise her that she can actually keep her home by filing a Chapter 13 bankruptcy instead.

In a Chapter 13 bankruptcy, the Trustee will NOT sell Jane's house to cover her $20,000 debt. Instead, he will allow Jane to keep her house, and will work with me, her attorney, to come up with a monthly payment plan that allows Jane to pay back just a small portion of her $20,000 debt over a period of three to five years. The rest of that debt will be wiped away.

Jane chooses to file a Chapter 13 bankruptcy rather than trying to go it alone and inevitably fall further and further behind on her mortgage payments. She is extremely happy and relieved to be able to keep her home.

Jane also appreciates something else about a Chapter 13 bankruptcy: she doesn't have to pay a lot of money up front to get her bankruptcy filed. She only has to come up with a few hundred dollars at the start to cover the court's filing fee and some required costs. The rest of the charges – her attorneys' fees – can be paid over the next three to five years, as part of her bankruptcy's monthly payment plan. This makes it a lot cheaper – and easier – for Jane to move forward and get out from under her debt burden.

A Word of Caution

In this book I am explaining common bankruptcy questions in the simplest terms in order to make complex financial issues easier to understand. But remember – bankruptcy law is actually very complicated and can be quite difficult, even for lawyers. There are some situations, for example, where a person who has equity in her house might be better off filing a Chapter 7 Bankruptcy by using exemptions provided for in the law.

It's important to remember that every person's financial challenges are unique and individual to their particular circumstances. Make it part of your strategy to talk to an experienced bankruptcy attorney to find out ALL your options for saving your assets and find out the details of what will and will not work for your particular situation.

CHAPTER 3
HELP – I'M BEING FORECLOSED!

Imagine her horror when Janice, a divorced mother of two, reads in the newspaper that her house is being foreclosed. She is frantic when she calls my office, terrified that she and her kids will soon be homeless.

When I meet with her later that same day, Janice tells me that she decided to keep the house after her divorce, so her kids could have some stability. But when her ex fell behind on his child support payments, she in turn fell behind on the mortgage.

In an effort to fix the problem, Janice paid a "loan modification company" two months' worth of mortgage payments for them to negotiate a loan modification through the Making Homes Affordable Plan. The problem is, once she paid them, they suddenly stopped returning her phone calls.

"The foreclosure is set for tomorrow," she says in tears. "Can you help me keep my home?"

My answer for Janice is "yes." In the vast majority of cases, bankruptcy can stop a foreclosure sale, so long as the sale has not yet happened. In fact, an experienced bankruptcy lawyer can file an emergency bankruptcy in less than an hour (although having more time than this is always much safer and less stressful).

Before her case to stop foreclosure can be filed, Janice will have to complete a one-hour credit counseling class online or over the phone. In addition, she'll need to provide bills from all of her creditors, including the mortgage company. This is so each creditor can get notice of the bankruptcy filing. Once the case is filed, I provide the bankruptcy case number to the mortgage company's lawyers and the sale is stopped. Janice and I then have two weeks to complete the rest of the bankruptcy documents: schedules, statement of affairs, and a plan.

In Janice's case – and in most cases involving potential foreclosure – I advise that the only real option for saving the home is to file a Chapter 13 bankruptcy, which will allow my client to cure the default by catching up on her mortgage payments over an extended period of time, usually three to five years.

During this time, Janice will be required to pay her ongoing mortgage payments as they come due, her regular monthly living expenses (food, gas, utilities, insurance, etc.), as well as any tax obligations.

Any leftover monthly income beyond these expenses is called her "disposable income," which must be paid over to the Chapter 13 Trustee for the three to five years that Janice is in bankruptcy. This "disposable income" payment will be used by the Trustee to pay the amount she is behind on her mortgage payments, as well as any tax debts she had at the time she filed bankruptcy. It will also be used to pay back a percentage of her other debts (credit cards, pay loans, medical bills, cell phone bills, etc.) as well as her lawyer's attorney's fees for handling her case.

The great news is that after Janice completes her payments over a period of three to five years, she will be current on her mortgage and taxes, and the balance of her unpaid debts will be discharged – wiped away. She won't ever have to pay them.

When she walks out of my office, Janice is relieved and hopeful. She is able to keep her home and she knows she's on her way to a fresh start.

Hope for Your Home

What about you?

Are you behind on your mortgage payments? Have you been sued for an amount that prevents you from being able to pay your mortgage? Do you have bills that prevent you from paying your monthly mortgage? Are you being foreclosed on?

If you are worried you may lose your home, be hopeful! Here are some concrete steps you can take to keep that from happening.

If you are just a month or so behind on your mortgage payments, try your very best to get current on them. Budget more carefully. Stop purchasing unnecessary items. Remember, the further you fall behind on your payments, the more you will eventually have to make up, and the harder and harder this will become.

If you are two or more months behind on your mortgage payment it's less likely you'll be able to catch up on your own. In this situation, you can contact your lender and ask them to work with you to create a rehabilitation plan. Your lender may be willing to modify or "re-cast" your loan.

This is when the bank adds the amount you are behind on your mortgage to the principal amount of the mortgage and gives you a new monthly payment amount. This takes care of any back payments you owe and brings you current on your payments. Sometimes, the bank can even modify the interest rate of your loan, so that your payments are actually lower than before. I've found that some people have success with this strategy, while others do not. It all depends on what your particular lender is willing – or not willing – to do.

Let me be clear, I am recommending that YOU contact your mortgage lender to attempt to modify your loan. Do not use a debt negotiation agency. Debt negotiation agencies are different animals entirely and I've found that these types of agencies often do not do what they say they are going to do and have gotten many of my clients into far more financial trouble than they were in before. I feel so strongly about this, that I have written an entire chapter later in this book to explain the possible pitfalls of these types of agencies. But for now, let me say this: it's usually best to steer clear.

Another excellent strategy for getting current on your mortgage is opting to file a Chapter 13 bankruptcy, which allows you to make back-payments on your mortgage over the course of a three to five-year repayment plan. The really helpful thing about filing a Chapter 13 bankruptcy that makes it the number one choice for many people is that it is a more comprehensive approach to debt that allows you get rid of other kinds of debt as well, including credit card bills, medical bills, car loans, etc.

Many of my clients have found that filing a Chapter 13 bankruptcy takes care of more issues – and bills – than just helping them get caught up on their mortgage payments. It's a more all-inclusive answer to their problems that gives them the "fresh start" they are looking for.

CHAPTER 4

WILL I LOSE MY CAR?

When filing bankruptcy, the answer is:

"Usually Not. Unless You Want To."

Meet Jennie. Jennie owes money on her Toyota Prius, which she bought because it gets great gas mileage and she wanted to help the environment. When she came into my office, Jennie owed more money on the Prius than it could be sold for, so I knew if she filed bankruptcy, the Trustee couldn't make any money on the sale of the car to help pay off Jennie's other debts. This meant that Jennie might be able to keep her car – but only if we could find enough money in her budget for her to make the car payments. Happily, we did just that, and Jennie was able to keep her car and get rid of her other debts by filing a Chapter 7 bankruptcy.

Another one of my clients, Doug, had too much equity in his motorcycle – that is, if he sold it he would have been able to make money on the sale. For this reason, if Doug filed a Chapter 7 bankruptcy, the Trustee would have sold it and Doug would have lost his vehicle. I advised him to file for Chapter 13 protection instead. This strategy allowed him keep his beloved ride.

A third client, Betty, had gotten herself into a situation where her car was only worth $5,000, but she still owed $20,000 on it. In her case, I counseled her to file a Chapter 7 bankruptcy. This allowed her to walk away from her car loan and no longer be saddled with that kind of debt.

After her discharge (usually about 90 days after a Chapter 7 bankruptcy is filed), Betty was able to purchase a new car. Her new loan rate was higher than she would have liked right after her discharge, but she chose a less expensive car and was able to handle her new payments because she no longer had any other debt.

As you can see, the strategy an attorney uses in filing bankruptcy is incredibly important. Filing the right kind of bankruptcy can mean the difference between being able to keep your vehicle and losing it. This is why hiring an *experienced* attorney matters.

What if My Car Has Been Repossessed?

Most people who walk into my office don't realize that filing bankruptcy can sometimes help them get their car back, *after* it's been repossessed.

Take Mark. Mark walks out of his house one Thursday morning only to discover that his car had been repossessed in the middle of the night. Mark has no idea how he is going to get to his job without his car. His friend gives him a ride to my office the very next day to get advice.

I tell him that if he files a Chapter 13 bankruptcy – as long as we file before the sale date for his car – he can get his car back. Moreover, he will not have to pay any repossession, towing, or storage fees involved in the repossession.

Within a couple of days of walking into my office, Mark has his car back and is able to drive himself to work again. I draw up a plan that allows Mark to pay off his car entirely over the course of three years as part of his Chapter 13 bankruptcy. The best part? In Mark's case, the plan takes care of his credit card and medical debts, too, and his monthly payments for *all* of his debts – including his car payment – is less than his car payment alone was before he filed for bankruptcy.

CHAPTER 5

WHAT ABOUT MY CREDIT SCORE?

Here's an astonishing fact: filing for bankruptcy can actually boost your credit score.

You read that right.

If that sounds too good to be true, consider this: credit bureaus look at what's known as "debt to income ratio" when determining a borrower's level of risk. When you get rid of your unsecured debt via bankruptcy, this ratio improves; hence, your credit score can also improve.

This isn't to say that bankruptcy is magic – that you will suddenly be able to buy your dream home or vehicle at amazing rates. But the idea that bankruptcy is a kind of death sentence for your credit rating or your ability to secure loans or buy property is a myth.

Take Jason, for example. Jason really needed a car after filing for bankruptcy. Why? His three-year-old went to daycare at one end of town, and his job was located clear across town in the exact opposite direction. Plus, he needed to drop off and pick up his child at his ex-wife's house 20 miles away every week. Without a car, his life would grind to a halt. Literally.

After filing strategically for Chapter 7 bankruptcy, Jason qualified for a car loan almost immediately after the discharge. His rates were not ideal, but he was out of debt and he got the car. He also qualified for a credit card.

With proper financial planning and dedication, Jason hiked his credit score back to 720 just 11 months after he filed for bankruptcy. He even managed to land a promotion at work that allowed him to telecommute and thus cut his weekly driving effectively in half.

Jason's story of rebuilding quickly after bankruptcy is not unusual. And that's because bankruptcy is NOT a scarlet letter you must wear for life. It's quite the opposite. Bankruptcy is a mechanism of hope, designed to give borrowers like Jason a fresh start and a chance to turn life around.

CHAPTER 6

DEBT NEGOTIATION AGENCIES

When someone asks me if they should try to get financial help from a debt negotiation agency (also known as a debt settlement company), the short answer is: I almost never recommend it. To explain why, let's start at the beginning: what is a debt negotiation agency?

Debt negotiation agencies are usually for-profit companies that make their money by attempting to talk their customers' creditors into taking less money than they are owed – for example, 50 cents on the dollar. Such agencies charge a fee for this service – most often a percent of the discount that is negotiated.

At first blush, this sounds great. Who wouldn't want to pay only half their debt back? But I've found that what sounds too good to be true is often just that – too good to be true.

I've worked with many clients who have paid thousands of dollars to debt collection companies only to find themselves even further in debt. Others find out too late that using a debt negotiation company significantly damages their credit for years into the future. How could these things happen?

Here's how: meet Keisha, a hairdresser who ran up $40,000 worth of debt on credit cards when she opened a beauty supply store – $30,000 on one card, $8,000 on a second card, and $2,000 on a third card. When Keisha realized she could no longer pay the minimum amounts on her credit cards, she decided to hire a debt negotiation agency to try to get herself get out of debt.

The debt negotiation agency told Keisha they would negotiate a discount with her credit card companies. Keisha would send monthly payments to the agency, which would pay off Keisha's credit cards, one at a time, until the discounted debt was paid. For their fee, the agency would also charge Keisha 20% of the amount they saved her – and they would collect that fee first, before beginning to pay off her credit cards. All Keisha had to do was send the monthly payment to the debt negotiation agency, instead of her credit card companies.

For her smallest credit card bill, the process seemed like it would work fairly well. The debt negotiation agency negotiated Keisha's $2,000 debt down to $1,000 for a 20% fee of $200. This sounded good – she would only have to pay a total of $1,200 on her original $2,000 debt.

Problem was, it didn't work out exactly like that. As planned, Keisha stopped paying all of her credit card bills so she could send the money directly to the debt negotiation agency instead. She paid the agency $400 each month; by the end of three months she'd paid them a total of $1,200. So far, so good.

But because Keisha hadn't been paying her $2,000 credit card bill directly to the credit card company, she racked up an additional three months' worth of interest, as well as an additional three months' worth of pretty steep late fee charges, totaling another $200. Still, the following month Keisha was able to pay that amount off, too. So, she only paid a total of $1,400 to pay off her $2,000 debt. Not bad.

What happened next *was* bad, though. While Keisha was paying off her small credit card bill, four months had gone by where she hadn't paid anything at all towards her $8,000 and $30,000 credit card bills. So of course, the credit card companies charged Keisha monthly interest and late fees on those debts as well – not to mention calling her constantly to try to collect the amount she owed. To the credit card companies, it appeared as if Keisha wasn't paying anything – because all of her payments had been sent to the debt negotiation agency.

It took Keisha two more months to send the debt negotiation agency enough money to cover their $800 fee for negotiating the $8,000 credit card bill, and an additional eight months to pay their $3,000 fee for negotiating the $30,000 credit card bill. (Remember, the agency had told Keisha that they were going to collect their fee first, before beginning to pay off her renegotiated debt.)

So, for a total of 14 months, Keisha didn't pay one single cent towards her two largest credit card bills – she just paid the debt negotiation company its fees.

During those 14 months, the credit card companies she owed money to went wild, calling and harassing Keisha constantly to try to force her to make payments – even when she'd already paid $4,000 in fees to the debt negotiation agency to supposedly help her get out of debt! To top it all off, the total amount she owed the credit card companies also kept rising, because she was being charged additional interest as well as late payment fees – every single one of those 14 months.

After she finally paid the debt negotiation agency $4,000 in fees, Keisha was still only able to pay $400 per month to pay off the $8,000 and $30,000 credit card bills. In order to pay off the rest of her debt, it would take Keisha four years – even at the 50% "discounted" rate. And that's not even including the amount of additional time it would take to pay off the interest and late fees that would continually keep accruing each and every month of those grueling four years.

A year into her payments, Keisha was still being harassed with calls from the credit card companies, even though she was doing her very best to pay back her debt to them. And with 4+ more years of the same looming in front of her, she felt like she wasn't making any progress. Using a debt collection agency hadn't made Keisha feel hopeful at all. Actually, she felt like she was at the end of her rope.

Moreover, because she'd gotten so many months behind on her credit card payments while she was paying the debt negotiation agency its fees, Keisha's credit score fell. And she heard that having a debt negotiation agency settle with multiple creditors for less than the original amounts could lower her credit score further and keep it there for many years after she'd paid off her debt at the discounted rate.

To top it all off, when she talked to her tax advisor, Keisha also found out that the $20,000 she'd "saved" by using the debt negotiation agency would have to be reported as income that she'd have to pay Federal and state income taxes on. Where was she going to find the money to be able to afford that?

That's what prompted Keisha to set up a free consultation with me. The bankruptcy option freed her of her consumer debt and allowed her to escape the seemingly endless cycle of stress and anxiety she'd been living with.

There were a couple other big plusses for Keisha when she decided to file bankruptcy. First, she wound up having to pay a MUCH smaller fraction of her debt than she had to pay using the debt negotiation agency – just $2,000 as compared to $20,000 with them.

Second, Keisha's bankruptcy plan allowed her to pay off her debt in three years as opposed to the four it would have taken with debt negotiation.

Third – and this was such a huge relief for Keisha – the moment Keisha's bankruptcy was filed, her creditors were barred by law from contacting her. This is called an "automatic stay" and it is one of the absolutely magical things about filing bankruptcy – virtually overnight, there are no more bills, no more collections letters, and no more annoying phone calls to deal with! For Keisha, this was a huge, welcome relief that completely changed her life. After her automatic stay went into place, she got a good night's sleep for the first time in years.

Fourth and finally, when she filed bankruptcy, the amount of debt she did not pay back was NOT counted as Keisha's income by the IRS. Therefore, Keisha avoided the thousands of dollars in tax liability she would have incurred if she'd stuck with the debt negotiation agency route.

These are the specific, important protections that the bankruptcy laws give to consumers: they allow debt to be wiped away or drastically lowered; debt is resolved in a reasonable amount of time according to a reasonable plan developed by a lawyer who represents you; harassing letters and calls and bills are controlled and stopped by law; and the amount you save through bankruptcy is not counted as additional taxable income.

Of course, not all debt collection agencies collect the total amount of their fees up front as Keisha's did – some keep a percentage of each monthly payment as their fee. While this would have allowed Keisha to begin paying off her debt sooner, her payment to her creditors each month would have been less, thus extending the amount of time it would take to pay off her discounted debt. But her credit score would still have taken a hit, she would still have been harassed by creditors for years, and she would still have to pay additional taxes on the amount she "saved." These are things that most people would rather not have to deal with.

To sum it all up, using a debt negotiation agency is risky at best. While some such companies are legitimate businesses, others are nothing more than scam artists looking to make a buck off of people who are already deeply in debt. I do not suggest taking the risk, especially when a Chapter 13 bankruptcy can do virtually the same thing with better financial results, more peace of mind, and better protections in place for the consumer.

Let's face it: most of us, when given our druthers, choose the path of least resistance when it comes to addressing our financial problems. It might seem easier at first to call a debt settlement company and have them somehow "take care of it" rather than take the time to find a qualified bankruptcy attorney and go through the legal process – but in the long run, it's not.

The bankruptcy process was created to protect consumers from being taken advantage of. It's a legal and carefully regulated process that our country provides so regular people can get out from under their debt when it's gotten to be too much to handle.

Using bankruptcy laws to your advantage is the smart thing to do when circumstances require it.

CHAPTER 7

CREDIT COUNSELING

Consumer credit counseling organizations are different from debt negotiation agencies. They are typically non-profit organizations that employ trained credit counselors who offer consumers information about credit, debt management, and budgeting.

Credit counselors can help you develop a debt management plan, but they typically cannot negotiate a reduction of the amount of debt that you owe – if you use them, you will still have to pay off the total amount of your entire debt.

Is going to a consumer credit counseling agency a good idea to try to avoid bankruptcy? Sometimes. There are certain circumstances where I recommend it to a person who has come into my office for advice, particularly when their debt is mild and confined to credit card debt only. But more often, I've found that credit counseling businesses can't help people who already have certain amounts or kinds of debt, and credit counselors generally send these people back to me for help.

As compared to bankruptcy attorneys, credit counseling businesses have some other additional limitations:

- They can't negotiate with the Internal Revenue Service (IRS),
- They can't help with state income taxes, real estate taxes, or car taxes,
- They can't help with your mortgage or foreclosure (to help you keep your house),
- They don't work with *all* credit card companies, and
- They usually don't work with credit unions.

If you are interested in credit counseling, it doesn't hurt to speak with a qualified bankruptcy attorney first to get the lay of the land and be sure you understand ALL your options. In fact, the bankruptcy laws require that all people who file bankruptcy also receive credit counseling – so my clients always receive this service when they decide to file bankruptcy with me. I always make sure to send them to a credit counselor that is recommended by the local bankruptcy court.

CHAPTER 8

IS BANKRUPTCY RIGHT FOR ME?

Here's a simple litmus test:

Debbie and Shonda both accrued serious credit card debt. When they come, separately, into my office, I asked each of them: "If you could no longer use any of your credit cards, starting today, would you be able to pay them all down within a reasonable timeframe?"

Debbie, who's struggling just to make her monthly minimums, says no. So, I would suggest she give strong consideration to the bankruptcy option.

Shonda, on the other hand, says that she could pay down the cards, but it would take planning and discipline. I would probably tell Shonda to explore other options before choosing bankruptcy.

The Bottom Line

The bottom line is that every person's financial situation is unique. Whether you have credit card debt, medical debt, a judgment against you, or car debt; whether you've lost your job or have been garnished or have had your income reduced; whether you've been through a painful divorce or recently lost your spouse – your pain is real. You deserve to be listened to and heard.

Sometimes, when you are in the middle of a difficult financial situation, it's hard to see the way out. That's why speaking to an experienced bankruptcy attorney is rarely a bad idea. It helps to talk through the situation with someone who truly knows the lay of the land to find out exactly what YOUR options are.

And if you go to an attorney who offers a free initial consultation, it won't cost you a single dime.

CHAPTER 9

CAN I FILE FOR BANKRUPTCY MYSELF?

There are many areas of law where I believe a non-lawyer might represent herself pretty effectively if she does a little research and proceeds carefully. Small claims court, child support, and simple landlord-tenant disputes are a few examples.

Bankruptcy, however, is not such an area of law. I always recommend a person hire an experienced bankruptcy attorney if he or she is going to file bankruptcy.

Why?

Take Rodrigo. Rodrigo was a natural-born entrepreneur – a self-made success story who started his own auto shop and built it from the ground up. But then a customer sued the business after an accident, claiming that Rodrigo's employee botched a brake inspection. Suddenly, Rodrigo found himself knee-deep in financial problems. Wisely, he chose the bankruptcy option. But unwisely, rather than hire a lawyer, he defaulted to the approach he knew best: "do it yourself."

What Rodrigo began to realize immediately is that bankruptcy law is incredibly complicated – even for lawyers. In fact, it's so complicated and specific that very few practicing attorneys "dabble" in bankruptcy law, like they might do in other areas of law. Lawyers know the truth: you either practice bankruptcy, or you don't. This is because bankruptcy is like no other area of law – there's too much you have to know to be able to "dabble" in it and do a good job.

Back to Rodrigo: as he proceeded to file bankruptcy on his own, he began to worry almost immediately that the vast amounts of paperwork he was filling out was incorrect. His wife, Paula, was worried too, afraid that if Rodrigo made a mistake they could lose their house or their cars – a very realistic fear.

Bankruptcy law is a technical and detail-oriented area of law – and the stakes are extremely high if something is missed, handled improperly, or strategized incorrectly. In every case, there are many calculations, worksheets, litmus tests, and exemptions that must be carefully weighed to determine which kind of bankruptcy will work for each person's unique situation. Many details are tracked in bankruptcy, even for a seemingly "simple" case. And if you get those details wrong – or if you just don't know the details that are needed in the first place – it can mean the difference between saving your house and losing it.

When Rodrigo went to court by himself, he accidentally showed up in the wrong courtroom. When he realized his mistake and found the correct courtroom, he discovered he'd missed his hearing. The worst part was that he had to wait a whole month before he could try again. Meanwhile, he just fell further into debt.

When Rodrigo finally went to court, the Trustee told him that he had filed for the wrong kind of bankruptcy. Rodrigo was frightened that he'd made a mistake he couldn't correct. The Trustee strongly suggested to Rodrigo that he consider hiring an attorney.

Rodrigo is not alone. I've often witnessed Trustees suggest to people attempting to file on their own that they hire an attorney. The reason for this isn't because they want them to have to pay more for bankruptcy. The reason is because the stakes are very high and they want the person's bankruptcy to be done right.

Another reason for hiring an experienced attorney is that different jurisdictions have different ways of handling bankruptcies which need to be taken into consideration and followed. While Federal law governs all bankruptcies, in some jurisdictions state exemptions apply instead.

Additionally, some judges and Trustees have more stringent and specific filing rules and requirements than others. This is especially true in the Western District of Virginia. Judges in different jurisdictions also often have different philosophies about bankruptcy, which might impact strategy in a given case.

Websites about bankruptcy just can't track or provide this kind of information because there is both a science and an art to the bankruptcy process. An experienced bankruptcy attorney who knows the ins and outs of the local system can maximize asset protection and get you the results you need.

Beyond getting results, having an experienced attorney can also help would-be "do-it-yourselfers" like Rodrigo by making them aware of other resources that are available. For example, if creditors have been coming into Rodrigo's shop after hours, hounding him, or leaving nasty messages, I can use laws like the Telephone Consumer Protection Act (TCPA) and the Fair Debt Collection Practices Act (FDCPA) to sue wrongdoers and collect money to pay for legal and filing fees and beyond.

I always tell people who are facing financial challenges to look at bankruptcy holistically, as a stepping-stone to a better life. You have one opportunity to get this right and break the downward spiral. You need to make sure it's done right.

When someone like Rodrigo comes to Slayton Law, we help him discharge his debts, free up resources to put groceries on the table, and get the fresh start he needs. Filing bankruptcy gives great hope to people – but only when it's done correctly.

CHAPTER 10

PHILOSOPHICAL OBJECTIONS

Our culture teaches us that truly resourceful people somehow find ways to "pick themselves up by the bootstraps" when things go south. Obviously, there is a lot to be said about self-reliance and resiliency. These are important and worthy values.

Ninety-nine percent of the people who walk into my office possess these values. Sadly, though, they often don't appreciate the extent to which external, systemic, and other negative forces have impacted their current financial situation. Instead of focusing their energy on hope for the future, many people spend a great deal of valuable time blaming themselves for their troubled past.

I see this as tragic for a few reasons. First, almost everybody I've ever known has made a bad financial decision or two at some point in their lives. If you get stuck in a cycle of blaming yourself for your debt, you may be more inclined to accept bad treatment from others (i.e. creditors), bad events (like the loss of your vehicle), and other bad results as some kind of "punishment" or karma that you imagine you "deserve."

This just isn't true – you don't deserve bad treatment, bad outcomes, or a bad future. Instead of beating yourself up for things that have happened in the past, it's important to focus on learning what your options are in the present and deciding how to move forward in the most productive and positive way possible.

Second, when you blame yourself, you're unlikely to act assertively to defend your interests and are more likely to fall into apathy or depression, which makes life – and dealing with your debt – that much harder. Action is a great remedy for apathy, depression, and fear in any area of life. I encourage you to harness the power of your own action by taking steps to know and understand all possible options that exist to solve your particular financial problems.

Finally, a negative, "self-blaming" attitude is likely to yield only short-term thinking that will fail to protect your long-term financial interests, such as your retirement assets. When it comes to finances, it's important not to allow temporary feelings of guilt or low self-esteem to get in the way of protecting your – and your family's – long-term financial health.

Consider Sal, for instance, a 48 year-old construction worker raising a family of three. Sal fell off a slippery ladder while painting his house and smashed four bones in his spine, making him unable to work. A bad reaction to his pain medication led to several additional hospitalizations and $60,000 in surprise hospital bills that his insurance decided not to cover. Even if you accept the proposition that it was partially Sal's "fault" for slipping off the ladder, that's a huge, outsized price to pay for a momentary lapse of attention.

Or what about Kassidy, whose husband deserted her on the eve of their fourth wedding anniversary, leaving her to raise their two children on her small bookkeeper's salary? Yes, it takes two to tango in any relationship, but sometimes things just don't work out between people. It's important for life to go on.

Or how about Paul and Catalina, victims of a financial scam that left them underwater on their house with no recourse in the U.S. courts, since the scam artists worked anonymously overseas? Does being taken advantage of in a gullible moment mean an elderly couple should lose their home? Of course not!

Public perceptions to the contrary, most people who file bankruptcy did not get into financial trouble by carelessly racking up credit card debt while shopping non-stop and leading hedonistic lifestyles. They just encountered bad luck or bad timing. Or, maybe, they made a few decisions that, in retrospect, were financially unwise.

In any case, while personal accountability and learning from your mistakes are important, it's equally – if not more – important to be able to let go of the guilt, so you can finally move in the direction of hope and get the help you need to move beyond what's happened to you.

Here are a few people you may have heard of who have used bankruptcy to secure their own futures:

President Donald Trump	Henry Ford
Dorothy Hamill	Walt Disney
Burt Reynolds	Toni Braxton
Dave Ramsey	Wayne Newton
MC Hammer	Cyndi Lauper

If they found hope in bankruptcy, so can you.

CHAPTER 11

CHAPTER 7 OR CHAPTER 13?

In general, there are basically two kinds of consumer bankruptcies that individuals can file: Chapter 7 and Chapter 13.

Many people qualify to file either. Some people only qualify for one or the other. The choice always depends on your individual financial situation. For this reason, it's essential to talk with an experienced bankruptcy attorney to find out for sure which type of bankruptcy fits your particular needs.

In this chapter, I want to give you some general information about the differences between filing a Chapter 7 and a Chapter 13 bankruptcy.

Chapter 7 Bankruptcy

A Chapter 7 bankruptcy is the shorter in duration of the two. It takes only about 90 days from filing to discharge and offers borrowers a chance to completely wipe away the debt they owe on credit cards, hospital bills, and other unsecured debts. Chapter 7 bankruptcy also discharges deficiencies you owe, such as balances due on repossessed vehicles or foreclosed homes.

Chapter 7 bankruptcies are often used to get rid of debt for people who have a minimum amount of assets or no equity in the home they own.

This doesn't mean that people who file Chapter 7 bankruptcies have to own nothing. Those who file under Chapter 7 are entitled to certain "exemptions." This means they are able to "exempt" some of the property they own from being used to pay off their creditors. A good bankruptcy attorney will be well-versed in these exemptions and will know how best to apply them to each person's unique situation.

Chapter 13 Bankruptcy

A Chapter 13 bankruptcy, on the other hand, gives you a chance to reorganize your debts, allowing you to protect larger assets such as a home while paying off a portion of your unsecured debts – often only 3-5% of the total amount you owe. One of the best things about a Chapter 13 bankruptcy is that it makes the process of paying back debt much easier because it stretches out your payments over the course of three to five years.

You and your lawyer develop a "plan" to pay off a negotiated amount that needs to be approved by the Chapter 13 Trustee and the bankruptcy judge. In this way, filing a Chapter 13 bankruptcy is similar to debt negotiation, but it's vastly safer and superior to that process because you don't have to negotiate with creditors to determine the amount of debt you will have to repay – the judge is the one who decides. And typically, the amount you have to repay is in the range of only 3-5% of your total debt, rather than the 50% or so offered by debt negotiation agencies (not including their fees).

After the court signs off on a Chapter 13 plan, the Trustee collects your payments each month during the three to five years of your plan and then divvies them up to pay your creditors. It's a process designed to help ensure your success in getting out of debt.

As I mentioned above, the Chapter 13 option is often used for debtors who are seeking to save a large asset, such as their home. The three to five year payment plan allows Chapter 13 filers who aren't current on their mortgage to catch up on payments over time.

And, if you owe more on your house than its current value, the Chapter 13 process can also effectively transform your second mortgage into unsecured debt and discharge it, so you'll only need to pay down the first mortgage.

Chapter 13 can also be useful for dealing with some types of IRS debts.

Which Kind of Bankruptcy is Right for You?

For the lay person, determining which kind of bankruptcy to file can be confusing, which is why having an experienced attorney's advice is vitally important.

For example, consider Rachel, who developed a medical condition that sapped her strength (and earning power). Slowly, she fell into debt and behind on her house payments. Soon, she was facing foreclosure.

Rachel thought she might be able to file a Chapter 7 bankruptcy to stop the foreclosure sale. Fortunately, she came into my office, just to make sure. At her free consultation, she learned that filing a Chapter 7 would delay the foreclosure, but not stop it entirely. With my advice and assistance, she filed a Chapter 13 bankruptcy instead and was able to save her home and landscaping business assets by paying a portion of what she owed to her unsecured creditors. Had Rachel chosen the Chapter 7 option, she would have gone over her allowed exemptions and lost her home.

Tanya's situation was different. She didn't own her home and hesitated to get information about bankruptcy because she was worried it would be too much of an ordeal. When she finally came into my office, I was able to tell her that a Chapter 7 bankruptcy could accomplish all of her goals and would only take about 90 days to complete.

Many people who walk in my door discover that they have the option to file a Chapter 7 or a Chapter 13. I advise them differently, based on their unique goals. I might recommend a Chapter 7 to people who value "getting things over with" over everything else. Or I might recommend a Chapter 13 to help a client avoid foreclosure and catch up on a number of missed mortgage payments. For others, it's a matter of how much they have to pay up front, or what they can afford to pay each month.

In each and every case, I advise my clients based on what their priorities and needs are, after I've listened to them carefully.

CHAPTER 12

PROTECTING YOUR RETIREMENT

Warren was proud to have $40,000 in his IRA and 401(k) plans after decades of saving. But when doctors diagnosed his wife, Sarah, with fibromyalgia and an immune system disorder, he raided these retirement accounts to pay for her medical expenses. Despite the best medical care, Sarah wound up having to quit her job due to her illness. On top of the loss of her income, the couple also had to pay fees and taxes for the early withdrawal of their retirement funds. Soon, Warren and Sarah found themselves unable to keep up with their everyday expenses and so they began accruing credit card debt. Eventually, they decided to file for bankruptcy to right the ship – but their retirement savings were long gone by the time they decided to do so.

It didn't have to be this way. If they'd gone to an experienced bankruptcy attorney *before* spending down their retirement account, they would have been able to keep all of their $40,000 using bankruptcy law to protect it.

Stories like Warren and Sarah's are tragic because retirement accounts such as pensions, IRAs, and 401(k)s are usually considered "exempt assets" under the bankruptcy code. In other words, creditors simply cannot go after what you've saved in those accounts.

Frustratingly, many people don't realize that they have this protection until after they've drained their retirement savings to pay their medical and other unsecured debts.

Whatever you do, get expert advice first, *before* you turn to retirement accounts to pay any of your debt. Your financial future will be much brighter if you do. That's what the bankruptcy laws are for.

CHAPTER 13

PROTECTING YOUR PRIVACY

Many of the people who walk into my office for advice are embarrassed by the idea of others in the community finding out they are considering bankruptcy.

Jamie, for example, is a very private person from a "respectable" family, and she worries about what might happen, not only to her reputation, but also to her career prospects if she chooses bankruptcy.

Here's the truth: Jamie's bankruptcy will go on the public record. All bankruptcies in the country do.

But I would argue that Jamie's concerns might not be warranted. First of all, the only way most people would ever find out that she filed bankruptcy is if Jamie herself decided to tell them. Jamie has control of who she decides to tell or not.

Second, for someone to find out independently about Jamie's bankruptcy, he or she would have to actively look for a record of it. Bankruptcies are generally not published in the newspapers. Frankly, most people are too busy or preoccupied with their own concerns, or just not interested enough, to go searching through the public records.

Lastly, and much more importantly, it's important to realize that bankruptcy should not be stigmatized! Bankruptcy law truly is a law of hope for citizens of the United States. It is an honorable option, provided by our country in the Constitution itself, to give worthy people a fresh start after hard times.

As I've mentioned before, many people you know about, including President Donald Trump, movie moguls such as Stan Lee and Walt Disney, celebrities like Larry King, Toni Braxton, Willie Nelson, Jerry Lee Lewis, and Marvin Gaye, and business executives like Henry Ford and Milton Hershey have all filed for bankruptcy when they needed it. There is no reason in the world why you should not use bankruptcy protection to your advantage, too. The bankruptcy laws were created to help people like you. That's their whole purpose.

Regarding Jamie's concerns, I would suggest that what other judgmental or catty people think about her is far less important than her ability to clear her debts, to stop living in fear of the phone and mailbox, and to create a path to a better, more hopeful, and more secure financial future.

Chapter 14

Bye-Bye Harassing Calls!

There is an amazing, fantastic, incredible watershed moment in the bankruptcy process that drastically improves the quality of life for many people who file bankruptcy. It's called the "automatic stay," and it instantly prevents creditors from directly trying to collect from you. They are effectively frozen out of your life. No more calls. No more statements. No more letters. No more wage garnishments. In fact, if a creditor has started a wage garnishment, it's stopped – almost immediately.

It's instant relief for my clients. By law, their creditors can no longer contact them. It feels like magic, but it's really another great example of how bankruptcy law works to protect consumers.

In 99 percent of cases, the automatic stay works like a charm. But in a few instances, creditors "don't get the memo" and keep calling or sending harassing letters to people they're barred by law from contacting. The good news is the law has teeth, and I can use it to stop creditors like these in their tracks.

In Aniqua's case, most of her creditors respected her bankruptcy stay, but one did not. Instead, he got really angry and started calling her at work and leaving rude messages on her voicemail. Aniqua had grounds to sue this creditor and recover damages. In other words, not only was the creditor compelled to stop, but he now also faced a judgment.

I love working for people like Aniqua – folks contending with harassment from creditors – because I know exactly how to stop such bad behavior and punish it in the courts, if necessary.

CHAPTER 15

HELP – I'VE BEEN GARNISHED!

I've found that, sadly, many people drag their feet and don't educate themselves about their financial options until circumstances become truly dire. Sometimes, they've thought about filing bankruptcy for a long time but have tried to "keep on keeping on." Then suddenly, the wages they depend upon to support themselves are garnished.

A wage garnishment is when a court orders a person's employer to withhold a certain amount of money from every paycheck that person receives. The court then takes the garnished money and sends it directly to the person or organization that is owed the money.

Eric received a much lower paycheck than usual when his wages were garnished because he owed child support.

Becca suddenly had 20 percent less money in her weekly paycheck when she was garnished for owing back taxes.

And, after months of considering filing for bankruptcy, Tom finally came into my office when his wages were garnished because of a court judgment against him.

It's not easy when you suddenly find yourself trying to make ends meet on three-quarters of your usual paycheck.

The good news is that when you file bankruptcy under the United States Bankruptcy Code – "The Law of Hope" – you don't have to live like this. Why? Because filing bankruptcy stops your paycheck from being garnished. Your employer will no longer be able to take money out of your paycheck.

When I explain this to my clients, they are thrilled. What's even better news is that I can often even get back money that has already been garnished. That's right, as long as we file the bankruptcy before the garnishment court date, we can get back the money that's already been taken. Talk about great news!

My only wish, as a bankruptcy attorney, is that people whose wages are on the verge of being garnished would come into my office *before* the garnishment actually happens. That way, I am able to help them keep money in their pocket and prevent it from being taken away in the first place.

CHAPTER 16

WHAT ABOUT MY IRS DEBT?

Most people believe that bankruptcy cannot wipe out IRS debt. In many cases, this conventional wisdom is correct. However, that's not always the case!

Consider Angel, who ran up a debt to the IRS while putting himself through school. Ironically, Angel was so afraid of accumulating crushing student loans that he chose to fall behind on his taxes rather than risk being burdened with loans.

Some people would automatically assume that Angel couldn't benefit from filing bankruptcy because his debt is with the IRS, but this isn't true. A good bankruptcy attorney will always carefully examine the details of each person's finances and debts in light of the relevant laws to determine whether that person might meet the standards to discharge at least some of his

IRS debt through the bankruptcy process. In Angel's case, if he filed his tax returns on time and waited over three years from the tax due date to file bankruptcy, then his IRS debts that are over three years old could actually be discharged in bankruptcy.

Even if Angel doesn't meet the standards to be able to discharge his IRS debt this way, he might still decide to file bankruptcy so that he can reorganize his debt. Filing for Chapter 13 can be an excellent and very effective way to manage a priority creditor like the Internal Revenue Service. I can devise a payment plan that lets Angel preferentially pay the IRS first, ahead of unsecured debt he owes to credit card companies, thus preventing the IRS from garnishing his wages or taking his assets.

CHAPTER 17

THE SLAYTON LAW ADVANTAGE

As someone dealing with financial issues of your own, you may have been taken advantage of by settlement companies, harassed by creditors, or blindsided by a huge medical bill or unexpected layoff. You likely feel protective of yourself and your family, and you need to be cautious about your next steps.

It seems to me that anyone in your situation should feel this way. Financial struggles are hard and emotionally draining. Deciding what to do next is a big decision and one that should not be taken lightly. You are worried about your home, your family, your assets, and your future. This is your *life*. Naturally, you don't want to trust it to just anybody.

As with any difficult situation, the most important first step is to figure out your options. That's the only way to be sure you are making the best decision for YOU. Hopefully, this book has been a good start in that direction.

But my guess is that you want more specific answers – answers that directly address your own particular circumstances. If this is the case, I recommend that you make an appointment to speak one-on-one with a highly rated, highly experienced bankruptcy attorney.

I'd be honored to be that attorney.

Why should you choose me and my team at Slayton Law as opposed to another bankruptcy law firm?

Here's what distinguishes what I do – and what my team does – for our clients:

OUR RATINGS ARE SUPERIOR

The lawyer you choose to provide you with legal advice should have high ethical standards and comprehensive bankruptcy knowledge. What's more, he or she should be able to back this up not just with words, but with actual *proof* in terms of awards and ratings.

Martindale-Hubbell

Martindale-Hubbell (associated with Lawyers.com) has awarded me an AV® Preeminent™ Rating – the highest rating possible:

What does an AV® Preeminent™ rating mean? According to the Martindale-Hubbell website, this award "recognizes lawyers for their strong legal ability and high ethical standards." An elite group of just 10 percent of all attorneys holds an AV Preeminent Rating, a designation trusted worldwide by buyers and referrers of legal services. I am proud to be part of this 10 percent.

It's important to note that lawyers cannot pay to get an AV® Preeminent™ rating. It has to be awarded. Martindale-Hubbell is one of the oldest legal rating organizations in the United States, pre-dating the internet era by many decades. The AV® Preeminent™ rating is bestowed on a lawyer only after a rigorous analysis of his or her ethics and legal ability. Many lawyers are not rated at all by Martindale-Hubbell, and others hold only a Notable or Distinguished rating. I am proud to have been deemed worthy by my legal peers to hold the highest rating possible.

Martindale-Hubbell is the rating system that most *lawyers* rely on to assess the legal ability of other lawyers. If lawyers use it to assess each other's legal ability, you should also consider it when choosing your attorney.

AVVO.com

AVVO.com is another website dedicated to rating lawyers and is meant to help consumers make the best decision in their choice of attorney. AVVO is relatively new, but has gained a great deal of popularity with many people in recent years. It is definitely worth looking at before choosing an attorney.

My Avvo.com Rating is 10 out of 10.

While Martindale-Hubbell's rating system is most useful in determining a lawyer's legal ability and ethical standards, the most useful thing about AVVO is its client review section. It's where lawyers' actual clients go online to rate their overall experience with the particular lawyer who has represented them. The reviews on AVVO cannot be purchased or controlled by lawyers, so it is an excellent place to find out what an attorney's clients think of his or her abilities.

There are two things to look for when you are looking at a lawyer's reviews on AVVO: quantity and quality. If you've ever purchased anything on Amazon.com, you know exactly what I mean.

First, quality. If a lawyer has consistently poor reviews from multiple clients, it raises red flags. It may be that she's not a very good attorney, or that she is a good attorney but doesn't give much thought to the client experience. Or, it could be something else that's harder to gage. The reviews themselves can give you some insight into what the issues may be, but it's best to proceed with caution if many clients are not having a good experience with a particular attorney.

Next, quantity. If a lawyer has great reviews but only has one or two of them, that may not be enough information for you to get a really good feel for exactly how satisfied that lawyer's clients truly are. Or, it may indicate a lack of experience on the lawyer's part. If on the other hand, a lawyer gets great marks from a large number of clients, it's more likely that attorney's clients are consistently satisfied. Naturally, no one will get perfect reviews from everyone, but that goes to show that the system of reviews is working the way it should.

I highly recommend that anyone who is considering meeting with me look at my clients' reviews on AVVO first. Why? Because there are a lot of them and they're really good!

Here are a few examples:

Excellent Service. Mr. Slayton provided excellent representation during my Chapter 13 hearing. My consultation with him proved to be informative. I was relieved to find out that help could be found for my financial situation. I will happily recommend Slayton Law, PLC to anyone that needs guidance and advice for their circumstance. – Shana, 2018

__Smart and Savvy Legal Expertise in a Relational Manner.__ Across the board, from the initial (free) consultation to our bankruptcy court date and even ongoing as we settle into our specific Payment Plan, Mr. Slayton provided my wife and I smart, savvy legal expertise in a genuinely relational and client-centered manner. We found Marshall to be equally adept at both the relationship aspect *and* the legal services aspect. He was sincere, warm, and relational as he counseled us by listening / understanding / assessing the particulars and variables of our family's situation. But he also knowledgeably explained and competently advised us on the legal particulars of bankruptcy options; the collection of important documents; how the process will unfold for us, including our day in court; and long-range thinking over the course of our Payment Plan. Because of the way he combined focused legal expertise on debt and bankruptcy with an attentive relational manner tuned precisely to our particulars and variables, my wife and I would highly recommend Mr. Slayton. –Nathan, 2018

Awesome Attorney. *Mr. Slayton was very upfront and honest with me from the beginning which I liked. The process didn't take months it was just a few weeks and everything was done.* –Arvonti, 2017

Positive Experience. *I had put myself in a horrible financial situation. After trying to work with a Debt Management company, (that only made my situation much worse), made the dreaded decision to file for bankruptcy. I met with Mr. Slayton to discuss my situation. There were a few hurdles along the way, but with Mr. Slayton's expertise, I feel like we worked through them with the utmost of ease. He is very informative, friendly, and very easy to work with. He never once made me feel like less of a person because of my situation. Of course, bankruptcy is the very last thing you ever want to think about, but after talking to him, I know I will be much better off in the end. If you are in need of a good attorney, I highly recommend Mr. Slayton.* – Melanie, 2017

The Best Bankruptcy Attorney. *My husband and I went to see a Bankruptcy lawyer and he was very rude and had short answers. So I kept looking around and several people recommended*

Mr. Slayton. I set up a consultation with him and he immediately explained everything I needed to know. Throughout the whole process he was very patient, understanding, and caring. If you are going to be filing Bankruptcy, I highly recommend Marshall Slayton. – Amber, 2016

Very Impressed. *This is our first time filing bankruptcy. We had no idea what we needed to do. We contacted Mr. Slayton and got right in to meet with him. We explained our situation and he guided us in right direction. He did all the work, all we had to do was get him the information he needed. At our hearing as we waited for our case we heard other cases being reviewed. Most all of them required more information, I was a little worried that ours would to[o]. We went up and she asked us about our case and said I have no more questions, everything is in order. That was such a relief! I highly recommend Mr. Slayton.* – Tracy, 2015

I am proud of my AVVO rating, but I am prouder still of my excellent client reviews. Why? Because my clients' experience matters a great deal to me, both when I am giving them advice in my office and when I am representing them in the courtroom. I understand from firsthand experience that financial struggles are not easy to deal with. I get a great deal of satisfaction knowing that the way I treat my clients makes a difference in their lives – and that the whole process is smoother and more comfortable for them as a result.

Google Plus Reviews

Another good source of client reviews that you should check out before speaking with any attorney is Google Plus. As of this writing Slayton Law has 39 reviews on Google Plus with a 4.9 out of 5.0 rating.

WE HAVE EXTENSIVE EXPERIENCE

At Slayton Law, we know that our many years of bankruptcy experience is invaluable to our clients.

My associate, Jennifer Wagoner, spent 14 years in the Chapter 13 Trustee's office for the Western District of Virginia before coming to Slayton Law. In the Trustee's office, Jennifer learned the important nuances of Chapter 13 filings which she now puts to work for the people who hire us. Her experience is invaluable to our firm, and she makes sure our clients' paperwork flows smoothly and is processed in a timely manner.

I've personally been practicing bankruptcy law for 25 years. I've served thousands of people from all walks of life and have helped get rid of many millions of dollars' worth of crushing debt. I am grateful for my experience because I put it to use every single day on behalf of each and every one of my clients.

I use this experience in the consultation room, when people come in to meet with me wanting to know the options that are available to them. It's second nature for me to explain and evaluate the options that exist for each person, because – after meeting with literally thousands of people through the years – I've pretty much seen it all. I've seen people at all different stages of their financial struggles. Most of all, I've seen what has worked and what hasn't worked for them. I use this knowledge every day to give the best advice possible to every person who walks through my door.

Happily, my experience has also been to see the tremendous relief people so often experience when they make the decision to file bankruptcy after struggling for so long. It is like a huge weight is lifted. This is why I love practicing bankruptcy – because I've seen no other area of law where clients get to experience such a wonderful sense of hope, relief, and renewal in their lives.

WE ARE ATTENTIVE LISTENERS

At Slayton Law, we see it as our job to listen to and really "get" our clients – where they're coming from, what their values are, and what they want to achieve.

When a person comes in for a consultation, we listen and ask questions to make sure we are truly understanding each person's individual situation. We know that many lawyers don't feel they have time to take this step, and instead go directly to giving advice. But we feel that we can only give the best advice after we understand what is most important to the people who are asking for it.

WE EXPLAIN EVERYTHING IN CLEAR, ACTION-ORIENTED LANGUAGE THAT IS EASY TO UNDERSTAND

Bankruptcy can be a wildly sophisticated and confusing process. The terms and ideas used can sound like a foreign language to people who have never had to deal with it before.

We pride ourselves on being able to translate "bankruptcy-ese" into normal human language. We make sure our clients understand the process as well as the final result.

At Slayton Law, we are extremely good at what we do. As I've said before, we've pretty much seen it all, and we understand exactly how to leverage the law and ethically maneuver through all the nuances of the process to get our clients the results they need.

WE HELP OUR CLIENTS DEAL EFFECTIVELY WITH CREDITORS

Creditors who do not follow the law and who bother our clients do not make us happy. We defend our clients' rights. Period.

WE PROVIDE ONGOING ASSISTANCE TO OUR CLIENTS

At Slayton Law, we can help you rebuild your credit score and equip you with resources to stay self-sufficient and thrive after bankruptcy.

We see bankruptcy law as more than just a job. It's a calling – a call to service, a call to help the unfairly disempowered, and a call to restore people's dignity and freedom.

We have the facility, the passion, and the track record to help you move from where you are now to where you want to be.

We have The Law of Hope.

CHAPTER 18

YOUR NEXT STEPS

Thank you for spending time with me and allowing me to pull back the curtain on the bankruptcy process and lay to rest some common misconceptions about how it works and what you can expect from it.

In exchange for your investment in time, I'd like to offer you a gift – the opportunity to come into my office and talk face-to-face with our team about your particular financial situation. Completely free. No strings attached.

We will dig down together and figure out what's really happening with your debt and what strategies you can use to reclaim your life. My goal is for you to leave my office more knowledgeable about your options and more hopeful about your future.

Simply call my office at 434-205-9035 to schedule your private, completely confidential consultation.

Whatever you decide to do, I encourage you to stay hopeful about your future, to learn about your options, and to take concrete action to get where you want to go.

I wish you the very best.

Sincerely,
Marshall M. Slayton
Slayton Law
434-205-9035

INDEX

Automatic Stay 43-44, 75-76

Automobiles see cars

AVVO 6, 12, 86-88, 91
  Ratings 6, 12, 86
  Reviews 86-91

Awards 6, 12, 84-85

Bankruptcy
  Chapter 7: 16, 18-19, 21, 29-30, 34, 63-65, 68-69
  Chapter 13: 18-20, 24, 28, 30-32, 46, 63, 65-69, 81, 88, 92-93

Cars 38-41, 43, 57, 63

Chapter 7 see bankruptcy

Chapter 13 see bankruptcy

Credit Counseling iii, 23, 47-49

Creditor Harassment 4,8-9, 13, 40-41, 44-45, 75-76, 82

Credit Score 33-35, 42, 45, 97

Debt Negotiation Agency iii, 27, 36-46, 47, 65, 66

Debt Settlement Company see Debt Negotiation Agency

Foreclosure 22-28, 64, 66

Filing With or Without Attorney 7, 21, 31, 46, 51-57, 64, 67-68, 70, 79, 80, 83, 86-88, 90

Free Consultation 13, 43, 51, 89, 98-99

Garnishment 75, 77-79

Google Plus Ratings 92

Hope i, 1, 5, 7-8,11-14, 16, 25-26, 35, 42, 57-58, 62, 73-74, 78, 83, 94, 97-99

Home iv, 1-2, 10, 15-20, 22-26, 33, 61, 64-66, 68, 82

IRS Debt 44, 48, 67, 80-81

Lawyers.com 84

Martindale Hubbell 12, 84-86

Preeminent Award 6, 12, 84-85

Privacy 3, 72-74

Pro Se fee Filing With or Without Attorney

Ratings 12-13, 83-86, 91-92
  Quantity and Quality 87

Retirement iv, 60, 70-71

Slayton Law ii, 11, 14, 57, 82-83, 88-94, 96, 97, 99
  Free Consultation 13, 43, 51, 89, 98-99

Wage Garnishment see Garnishment